The Night

by Mark Murphy

First performed at the Traverse Theatre, Edinburgh, on
4 August 2005, and at BAC, London, on 31 August 2005

The Night Shift

Writer and Director	**Mark Murphy**
Performers	**Catherine Dyson**
	Jason Thorpe
Designer	Miranda Melville
Composer	Nathaniel Reed
Lighting Designer	Lizzie Powell
Relights	Adam Bullock
Technical Management	Adam Bullock and Lizzie Powell
Marketing and Press	Dan Pursey @ Mobius Industries
Photography	Sheila Burnett (*cover image*) and Pau Ros
Print Design	David Hardcastle @ Rubbaglove

Mark Murphy's work is produced by

Commissioned by

  warwick arts centre COVENTRY

Isle of Wight

Developed at BAC

Funded by

Fuel
BAC, Lavender Hill, London SW11 5TN
tel 020 7228 6688   *fax* 020 7978 5207
e-mail info@fueltheatre.com
www.fueltheatre.com

Biographies

Mark Murphy (Writer/Director)
Mark Murphy is an award-winning director, writer, filmmaker and movement specialist. As founder and director of Vtol Dance Company, between 1991 and 2001, he directed seven major shows – all touring extensively throughout the UK and Europe. He has co-directed two acclaimed theatre productions for The Northern Stage Ensemble: *A Clockwork Orange* and the award winning *1984*, both utilising Mark's signature mix of film and live performance. He is an associate director for Walk The Plank and directed their collaboration with Australian company Bambooco for the Manchester Commonwealth Games, conceived and directed their highly-praised production *S.W.A.L.K.*, and many large-scale, site-specific projects. Mark has written two plays: *A Wing and a Prayer* and *The Night Shift* and two screenplays. He has also received a Peggy Ramsay Award for his writing. Recently he was filmmaker and movement director for *Julius Caesar* with the RSC and will be working in late 2005 with Legs On The Wall in Sydney.

Catherine Dyson (Performer)
Catherine Dyson is a performer, deviser and writer. Most recent theatre work includes *The King & I* (BAC) and *Dead Man's Biggest Fan*, which has been selected for the 2005 This Way Up touring initiative. She has co-written a number of plays including an adaptation of *Titus Andronicus*, in which she also played the part of Lavinia. Other roles include Alice in *Alice in Wonderland*, Angustius in *The House of Bernarda Alba*, and several ghostly appearances as The Woman In Black.

Jason Thorpe (Performer)
Jason's theatre credits include *World Cup Final 1966* at BAC, *His Dark Materials* at the National Theatre, *Monkey* at the Young Vic, The Clod Ensemble's *Greed*, Told by an Idiot's *Shoot Me in the Heart*, *Servant of Two Masters* at the Sheffield Crucible, *Grimm Tales* at Leicester Haymarket, *Peter Pan* at the National Theatre, Hideki Noda's *Red Demon* in Tokyo, and *Princess Sharon* for Scarlet Theatre Company. TV credits: *Rose and Malloney* for Company Pictures, *Margaret* and *Armstrong and Miller* for Channel 4, *Goodbye Mr Steadman* and *The Wire in the Blood* for ITV, and *The News Never Sleeps*

for Talkback. Jason starred in the title role in both series of the BAFTA-nominated *Sir Gadabout* for ITV. Film credits: *Nine Lives of Thomas Katz* and *Jack and the Beanstalk: The Real Story* for Jim Henson Productions and *L'Inspiration* for No Egos Required Film Festival.

Miranda Melville (Designer)
Miranda Melville has designed extensively for theatre, opera, film and dance. Recent work includes *How to Live* with Bobby Baker at the Barbican Theatre and *Jardin Blanc* for Yolande Snaith Dance Theatre. Her long collaboration with Mark Murphy includes many designs for Vtol Dance Company and *A Wing and a Prayer*.

Nathaniel Reed (Composer)
Nathaniel Reed studied Performing Arts at Middlesex University. He has composed for theatre, dance and film. Collaborations include work with Vtol, Frantic Assembly, Cardboard Citizens, Jeff Noon, Kip Hall, and Liam Steel. He is currently working with Panta Rei Danseteater.

Lizzie Powell (Lighting Designer/Technical Management)
Lizzie trained at LAMDA in Stage Management and Technical Theatre (2000–2002) and is currently a director of the Irish theatre company Blood In The Alley. Lighting Designs for Blood In The Alley include *Tricky* at the Richmond Studio Theatre and King's Cross, London; *This Ebony Bird* at The Half Moon Theatre, Cork; *Romeo & Juliet* at Belvedere College, Dublin; Cork Opera House; *The Black Box*, Galway; and *Second City Trilogy* at The Half Moon Theatre, Cork. Her credits for Liquid Theatre include *Cowboy Mouth* at BAC, London; *Crave* at BAC and on national tour; *Patching Havoc* at Latchmere Theatre, London; and *The Cudgel and The Rapier* at BAC.

Adam Bullock (Relights/Technical Management)
A freelance lighting designer and production electrician for theatre and events, Adam has recently completed an Associate LD role on the West End musical *Hedwig and the Angry Inch* and a Scandinavian tour of *Jesus Christ Superstar*. A regular with the English Pocket Opera Company, Opera Holland Park and event production teams, his design, relights and production credits span all sectors of the industry.

The Night Shift

A dark thought – could I write? The path from choreographer to writer is not exactly well trodden, is it? I had a shed to write in, a computer to write with and a single sentence in thick, black marker-pen stuck to the top of my computer screen but could I actually write? She would wake with a scream – I knew that, but was that writing?

The Night Shift was conceived at a time of enormous change in my life as I had until that point made large-scale, theatrical dance pieces with my company Vtol. My frustration with using movement as the primary means of communication, had already led me to incorporate film and other people's writing with great success but by 2001, my desire to tell stories by other means had become so strong that I took the decision to close my company at the height of its powers. But could I write?

David Lynch talked about sitting very still and allowing his subconscious to fall through a series of trap doors, going ever deeper into an idea. I now felt the wind whistling in my ears, as the first door dropped – 'an anaesthetist who can't sleep!' Later, a little light research led me to *parasomnia*: a condition encompassing everything from sleepwalking to sleep homicide. The part that really fascinated me was most people's dream state is accompanied by paralysis, whereas the *parasomniac* bypasses the paralysis stage and is then condemned to act out their dreams. I then wrote:

'Aaaaaaaaaaaaaaaaaarrrrrrrrrrrrrrrrrrrrrggggggggggggggghhhhhhhhhhh! Oh, hello. Am I asleep? If I am, okay, but if not, what's this? It could be a dream about a dream or I could be you dreaming that I'm dreaming that you're awake. Then again, I could be awake. If so, what are you doing here? And more worryingly, if I'm asleep, why are you watching me? As I said – I don't know and now you don't either. Not a bad place to start though.'

I was invited by BAC in London to try the show as part of *SCRATCH*, a programme designed to test new ideas without the pressure of having a completed show and in October 2003, *The Night Shift* clocked on. As often happens with time, the glare of lights peeled away the gloss coat and deeper themes revealed themselves. An anaesthetist who can't sleep was a catchy hook, but that's all. What shone through was a woman acting out an incident from very early in her life. An incident that now intruded on her dreams and over the next six months, I set about finding it. One thing that wouldn't change was her climactic scene. For the first and only time in my life I wrote this scene in one, short sitting without subsequent revision or alteration. It wrote itself; all I did was press the keys as the authentic voice of a child whispering in the night poured out without censor.

As I re-drafted, a complex structure began to simplify. A woman with a sleep disorder and her much put upon lover. An older, troubled man in a secure unit and his newly qualified, female counsellor. Multiple trap doors exposed symmetrical identities on unavoidable and terrifying trajectories. I now stared at ninety-three pages and the ever-present sentence written on my computer in thick, black marker-pen:

You are only free to face the future once you have confronted your past.

The walls of my shed felt like they were closing in. A new, dark thought surfaced – what have I written?

Mark Murphy, 2005

fuel

Fuel is a producing organisation, formed by **Louise Blackwell**, **Kate McGrath** and **Sarah Quelch**. It works in partnership with artists to develop, create and present new work for all ages, particularly in the field of live performance. Fuel is currently working with Gecko, Mark Murphy, Patter, Sound&Fury, The Clod Ensemble and Will Adamsdale.

Very special thanks to:

Eric MacLennan, Craig Conway, Jon Linstrum, Terence Mann and Julian Rounthwait who worked on *The Night Shift* during its development.

Special thanks to:

Arts Admin, Matt Applewhite, Niall Black, Sheila Burnett, Nick Cave, Laura Collier, Neil Darlison, Niamh Dowling at Manchester Metropolitan University, Richard Dufty, Sean Egan, Paul Elliot, Maria Foran, Anneliese Graham, Mike Griffiths, David Hardcastle, Pete and Rowena Hayward, Nick Hern, Mark Hillier, Phillip Howard, David Jubb, Andrew Laing, Gloria Lindh, Phyllida Lloyd, Ron McAllister, Tamsyn McLean and Scott Dickson, Mum, all at Mobius Industries, Tom Morris, Stephen Munn, Caro Newling, Greg Piggot, Liz Pugh and John Wassel at Walk The Plank, Alan Rivett, Helen Roberts, Pau Ros, Stage One, Nick Starr, Emma Stenning, Annette Stone, Steve Wald and Suzanne Walker.

THE NIGHT SHIFT

Mark Murphy

For Maria

Characters
ALICE
GRAY
HELEN
ANDREW

INT. BEDROOM – NIGHT

A large curtain is closed and obscuring the stage. A sleepy ALICE *slowly draws back the curtain, revealing herself and a double bed in the centre of the room. She yawns, stretches, undresses and calmly gets into bed.*

From offstage a phone rings. ALICE *sits up grumpily.*

ALICE (*to herself*). Oh Gray.

>*She gets up and disappears out of the doorway. We hear her answer from offstage.*
>
>(*Offstage.*) Gray . . . I was aslee . . .
>
>*A beat.*
>
>Who's that? For what . . . is it? What is?
>
>*A beat.*
>
>Listen, I don't know who you are, so go away . . . leave me alone.
>
>*A beat.*
>
>Who?!
>
>*A beat.*
>
>You have the wrong number you have the wrong number you have the wrong number you have the wrong number.
>
>*A beat.*
>
>You have the wrong fucking number.
>
>*A beat.*
>
>For what?
>
>*A beat.*
>
>Leave me alone.
>
>*The offstage phone goes dead.*
>
>ALICE *re-enters from a different doorway. She looks confused, like someone has moved her bed. She flops back into it and pulls the cover up over her head.*
>
>*After a moment,* ALICE*'s boyfriend* GRAY *enters. He takes off his coat at the door then watches her sleeping for a moment before moving to the bed.*
>
>ALICE *senses something and suddenly yelps, jumps and jackknifes halfway out of the bed. She tries to focus on the figure looming over her.*

Gray! What are you doing? Fucking hell, you scared me.

GRAY. Morning. You want some tea?

ALICE. How did you get in?

GRAY sits on the bed.

GRAY. The key you gave me?

ALICE. I know . . . but.

She holds his face.

How can I put this?

GRAY. Don't just turn up without warning you?

ALICE. Try 'Don't hover over me like a fucking serial killer.'

GRAY laughs.

GRAY. I see what you mean.

ALICE. Yeah?

GRAY. Yeah.

ALICE grumpily pulls the quilt up over her head. GRAY rewinds out of the room, taking his coat with him.

He then re-enters and repeats the same actions. ALICE jumps again.

ALICE. Gray! What are you doing? Fucking hell, you scared me.

GRAY. Morning. You want some tea?

ALICE. How did you get in?

GRAY sits on the bed.

GRAY. The key you gave me?

ALICE. I know . . . but.

She holds his face.

How can I put this?

GRAY. Don't just turn up without warning you?

ALICE. Try 'Don't hover over me like a fucking serial killer.'

GRAY laughs.

GRAY. I see what you mean.

ALICE. Yeah?

GRAY. Yeah.

GRAY exits and then enters immediately.

Honey . . . honey?

She stirs a little.

Hello . . .

She rolls over.

You want some tea?

She wakes this time with less of a fright, but still with surprise.

ALICE. Gray! What is going on? How did you get in?

GRAY *sits on the bed.*

GRAY. The key you gave me three weeks ago?

ALICE. I know . . . but.

She holds his face.

How can I put this?

GRAY. Don't just turn up without warning you?

ALICE. That's a start.

GRAY. Yeah?

ALICE. Yeah.

ALICE *slumps back under the covers.* GRAY *jumps back up and exits. Without a pause, he's flying back in – coat off, striding to her and flopping onto the bed. The words are spoken fast.*

GRAY. Honey . . . honey? You want some tea, sweetheart?

ALICE. Gray!

GRAY. What!

ALICE. How did you get in?

GRAY. You gave me a key, remember?

ALICE. I know . . . but.

She holds his face.

How can I put this?

GRAY. Don't just turn up without warning you?

ALICE. Try 'Don't hover over me like a fucking serial killer.'

GRAY. I see what you mean.

ALICE. Do you?

GRAY. I do.

ALICE. Yeah?

GRAY. Yeah.

He's gone again and then back in, heading for the bed.

You want some tea?

She wakes shaking her head.

ALICE. Gray! What are you doing?

GRAY. You look tired.

ALICE. I'm asleep.

She squirrels back under the quilt. GRAY *exits.* ALICE *then pokes her head out like a meerkat and looks around.*

Ugh?

She gets up, checks the door and then paces back to the bed. The moment she pulls the quilt over her head, she wakes with a truly horrific scream.

Aaaaarrrrggghhhhhh!

ALICE *stares blankly at the audience.*

Oh fucking hell, hello. Did you see that? Shit, you did. All of it? Well, which bit?

A beat.

I've got some explaining to do, haven't I?

She gets up.

Listen, I've got this thing. I won't bore you with the details, but it's a sleep thing. So, what you saw, or you think you saw, was a dream. That was all a dream. This is real.

A beat.

Hold on a minute.

She turns away and slaps her own face.

Am I asleep? I might look awake but you see, I don't know. Do you start to see the problem. This could be a dream as well or a dream about a dream or I could be you dreaming that I'm dreaming that you're awake. But I am awake, I think. As I said – I don't know and now you don't either.

She smiles.

Not a bad place to start though, is it? Sorry. How rude of me. My name's . . . fuck. What's my name?

She stands right in front of a man on the front row.

What's your name?

The man will answer 'whatever', but ALICE *carries on regardless.*

Alice. Nice. What a lovely name, I like that. You see, I could be Alice. I have no idea. Really.

She smiles manically and then spins around.

Shush! Wait, let me show you something.

She swishes the curtain shut.

Scene change:

INT. SECURE UNIT, SESSION ONE – DAY

ANDREW *re-opens the curtain from the opposite side. Early fifties with more than a passing resemblance to* GRAY, *he moves to his neatly made bed and smooths down a non-existent crease.*

HELEN *enters. Youngish, thin and easily mistaken for* ALICE. *She is immaculately groomed in a professional suit and for a moment, she just looks and smiles enigmatically at* ANDREW*'s back.* ANDREW *doesn't move. She then unfolds a wooden chair and places it upstage left. They are as far from each other as is physically possible. There's a little stand-off before* ANDREW *speaks.*

ANDREW. Well?

She continues to smile pleasantly at the back of his head.

Who this time?

HELEN. Andrew.

ANDREW. That's my name.

She smiles some more.

HELEN. How are you?

ANDREW. What's going on?

HELEN. I've been asked to come in and talk to you, Andrew.

ANDREW. Talk to me. Nice. Therapist then.

HELEN. Not exactly. I'm here to help you, Andrew.

ANDREW. Right.

HELEN. And to help you help yourself.

ANDREW. I don't need any help to help myself.

HELEN. We're worried about you, Andrew.

ANDREW. Are we? Who is we?

HELEN. We care.

ANDREW. Well, tell 'we' not to worry, I'm fine.

HELEN. Does my visit trouble you?

ANDREW. Not in the slightest.

HELEN. This is by way of an introduction, you see. We can start in a few weeks . . . if you want?

ANDREW. Start what?

HELEN sits up straight. She likes this question.

HELEN. Your work, Andrew. Your work.

ANDREW snorts and shakes his head.

Before our next session . . .

ANDREW. If there is one.

HELEN. Yes. I want you to practise saying something.

ANDREW. Do you?

HELEN. I do. I want you to practise saying . . . ready?

ANDREW. Ready.

HELEN. 'I will do all I can to help myself get well and will allow others to assist me in that goal.'

For the first time, ANDREW *looks around at* HELEN.

ANDREW. And do you want me to do it in that voice as well?

She smiles and gets up to leave.

HELEN. Very good, but. Consider the possibility that we have more in common than you think, Andrew.

ANDREW. What's your name?

She smiles.

HELEN. See you in a month. And before you say it, that's not my name.

ANDREW (*sarcastic*). I look forward to it.

She leaves and although gone from sight, ANDREW *can still hear her heels up the corridor. When they clip-clop no longer, he then repeats* HELEN's *little mantra.*

I will do all I can to help myself get well and will allow others to assist me in that goal.

He slowly draws the screen closed.

I will do all I can to help myself get worse and will allow others to assist me in that goal.

It's closed.

Scene change:

INT. BEDROOM – THE NEXT DAY

ALICE *enters with the curtain still closed.* GRAY *bangs and then shouts from outside.*

GRAY (*offstage*). Alice! Can I come in?

ALICE (*offstage*). Only if you do what I said.

GRAY (*offstage*). No way.

ALICE (*offstage*). You promised.

GRAY (*offstage*). Not *that* I didn't, it's embarrassing.

ALICE (*offstage*). Fine. You can't come in then.

GRAY (*offstage*). Fine.

ALICE (*offstage*). Fine.

GRAY (*offstage, shouting*). Fine!

ALICE (*offstage*). Fine.

Silence, then GRAY *cracks.*

GRAY (*offstage*). Alright! I'll do it, anything.

ALICE (*offstage*). Anything?

GRAY (*offstage*). Let me in, it's fucking freezing!

She finally opens the curtain. GRAY *blunders in.*

ALICE. Good. Now, let's do the practice, so we're both clear.

GRAY. You're serious, aren't you?

ALICE. Yes, do the rehearse.

GRAY. 'Yeah, dooo the rehearse.' Look, I could just promise not to sneak in on you again.

She kisses him.

ALICE. You stand there and pick up the phone.

She pushes him into the corridor.

GRAY. But there isn't a phone.

ALICE. I know. Try acting.

She slaps his arse and relocates downstage.

Ready!

GRAY *is shaking his head.*

GRAY. Erm. (*Deep breath in.*) Okay . . . hello Alice.

ALICE (*shouting*). Hello Gray.

GRAY. I was thinking of coming over.

ALICE (*shouting*). Great.

GRAY. Yeah? Erm . . . yeah, coming over. Oh, fuck it.

GRAY comes in to talk.

I got that wrong, didn't I?

ALICE. You did. Ask me if it's okay, then tell me a time. The order's important.

GRAY. Yeah, sorry.

He scurries off.

(*Shouting.*) Is that okay?

ALICE rushes back to the corridor.

ALICE. Gray! Go from thinking of coming over.

GRAY. Sorry.

She returns to her place.

I was thinking of coming over.

ALICE. Great.

GRAY. Is that okay?

ALICE. Sure.

GRAY. About . . .

He checks his non-existent watch.

. . . ten thirty?

ALICE. Perfect. See you then. You will knock?

GRAY. Knock. Yes.

GRAY takes an imaginary phone from his ear and then looks at his hand.

Fucking hell.

They meet in the middle.

ALICE. See, easy.

GRAY is laughing now.

GRAY. If a little odd.

ALICE. I'm only playing.

GRAY. At?

ALICE. Just testing your resilience.

GRAY. For?

ALICE *grabs hold of him.*

ALICE. Let's go to bed.

ALICE gets quickly into bed while GRAY undresses.

Come on.

GRAY. I'm thinking.

ALICE. I know, I can hear you. About?

GRAY smiles.

GRAY. You don't want to know.

ALICE. Try me.

GRAY. I'm thinking . . . nah.

ALICE. Gray!

He smiles at her but keeps his counsel.

I know what you want me to say.

GRAY. Say it then.

ALICE. You say it.

GRAY. Fucking hell.

He stands and announces.

I love you.

ALICE laughs.

ALICE. You're pissed.

GRAY throws a sock at her.

GRAY. I think you love me.

ALICE. You love you.

GRAY. Nothing wrong with that.

He jumps in beside her.

Well?

ALICE. I like you.

GRAY. Alright, that'll do. For now.

She kisses him as the lights fade. They sleep.

A little while later, GRAY gets up to go to the loo. While he's out, ALICE sits up and then gets up. She looks a little out of it, as she stands quite still, looking into the middle distance.

A toilet flushes offstage and then GRAY groggily comes back.

I wouldn't go in there for a bit.

She doesn't respond.

Can't you sleep?

Still nothing.

Another test?

ALICE *is now standing at the foot of the bed.*

Hun?

ALICE. Bare, cracked concrete and a path with mint overgrowing. Lupins.

She half-turns to GRAY.

They said last summer was the hottest in living memory.

GRAY *passes his hand across* ALICE*'s unblinking eyes.*

GRAY. Alice . . . Alice?

ALICE. Crazy paving.

She walks away from him.

A swing next to the new window. The one that Heather Trim swung too high on and tipped over. We had to put tent pegs on the back legs to hold it down.

She looks straight at GRAY.

. . . I tried to buy tent pegs from the Paki shop and he thought I said another word and gave me Tampax.

GRAY *can't help laughing.* ALICE *scuttles past him.*

The wind blows and there is alyssum growing in tight white bunches at the bottom near the cross of my goldfish, who they said escaped and was then callously run over. We have an extension with two inside-out tyres painted white with dead plants in.

More little steps.

We have the first SodaStream in our street. It makes pop. It's amazing.

GRAY. Let's get back into bed, Alice.

GRAY *tries to guide her over to the bed. She shrugs him off and then flips instantly into awake mode.*

ALICE. Can't you sleep? You too hot?

GRAY *studies her.*

GRAY. Yeah.

ALICE. I need some water, do you want some?

GRAY. No.

She gets to the door.

ALICE. Have you had a shit?

GRAY. Yeah . . . sorry.

> ALICE *walks out.* GRAY *sits on the bed and looks understandably thoughtful. He gets up, shaking his head and then slowly closes the curtain.*
>
> *Scene change:*

INT. SECURE UNIT, SESSION TWO – EVENING

HELEN *opens the screen with a flourish, spreading light into the room.* ANDREW *is at the foot of the bed, with his hands folded around the back of his head.*

HELEN. Good evening, Andrew.

ANDREW. You came back.

HELEN. Is that a surprise?

ANDREW. I'm amazed.

HELEN. How are you?

ANDREW. I'm doing all I can to help myself get well, allowing others to assist me in that goal.

HELEN. You seem upset?

ANDREW. You're good.

HELEN. Where is the pain?

ANDREW. In the arse.

HELEN. What do you need?

> ANDREW *takes his head out of his hands.*

ANDREW. Who are you and why have you come back?

> HELEN *sits on the wooden seat a little closer to the bed than last time.*

HELEN. Let's start this again.

ANDREW. If you wish.

HELEN. I'm part of a voluntary organisation that is trained to intervene in cases like yours. I have a background in clinical psychology and this is also part of my study.

> ANDREW *shudders.*

ANDREW. Voluntary organisation. God squad then. What is it? 'Do not be afraid of any man, for judgement belongs to God.'

HELEN. My personal beliefs are really of little importance.

ANDREW. Lovely.

HELEN. I'm not here to judge you, Andrew. I am here to help you.

ANDREW. Why would you judge me?

HELEN. I'm sure you're judging me.

ANDREW. I know nothing about you, not even your name.

HELEN. I think it's important to start with a clean slate.

ANDREW *warms to this. He sits a bit closer to her on the bed.*

ANDREW. Okay, let's get it out in the open. What do you know about me?

HELEN. I know your name is Andrew, obviously. I know about your problems with alcohol dependency. I've been told a little about your depression and that you may be at risk of harming yourself.

ANDREW *moves away again.*

ANDREW. And the rest.

HELEN. That's all I know.

ANDREW. Oh really?

HELEN. That's it.

ANDREW. Look, I get this bullshit on a daily basis, so don't be offended if I ask you to leave.

HELEN. You can rely on me, without hesitation, to tell you the truth.

ANDREW. How do you respond to someone who promises to tell you the truth? Do you not think the truth should be a given, and in fact only a liar would promise it?

HELEN *sits back and thinks.*

HELEN. You have a point but the circumstances that bring us together perhaps . . .

ANDREW *cuts her off then counts on his fingers.*

ANDREW. Yeah, yeah, alright. So. The booze, the sadness, the risk. That's all you know about me?

HELEN. Yes. Whatever else there is, is up to you to tell me.

ANDREW. Really?

HELEN. Yes Andrew. There is a bond of confidentiality to protect us both. Those are the rules and we take them very seriously.

ANDREW *gets up.*

ANDREW. Me too, good. The rules are the rules. It's a serious thing. Right, can I start this again?

HELEN. How would you like to do that?

ANDREW. Could you come in again?

HELEN. Physically?

ANDREW. Yes. I'd like to start again, you know, with a clean slate.

HELEN. Good for you.

HELEN gets up to leave.

ANDREW. This might seem a little odd, but could you do the screen as well? The order's important.

HELEN. Of course.

She pulls it almost shut and then turns to ANDREW.

It's Helen, by the way.

It's closed.

Scene change:

INT. BEDROOM – MORNING

The curtain stays closed as GRAY suddenly moans from behind it.

GRAY (*offstage*). Urrarrgh . . .

ALICE (*offstage*). Gray?

GRAY (*offstage*). Urrgh . . . need . . . need to get her bottle . . .

ALICE (*offstage*). Wake up, babe, you're having a dream.

GRAY (*offstage*). . . . needs changing . . . I'll do it, you sleep . . . I'll do it . . .

ALICE (*offstage*). Gray!

He comes to.

GRAY (*offstage*). What? What is it?

ALICE (*offstage*). You had a dream.

GRAY (*offstage*). Did I?

A beat.

What time is it?

ALICE (*offstage*). Nine.

A beat.

What did you dream?

GRAY jumps out of bed.

GRAY (*offstage*). Fuck! I'm late.

ALICE (*offstage*). You are.

GRAY (*offstage*). Thanks.

> GRAY *runs around in the dark trying to find his shoes. He half-trips and then attempts to open the curtain.*

Can I open the curtains?

ALICE (*offstage*). Don't you dare!

GRAY (*offstage*). Can I turn the light on then?

ALICE (*offstage*). No!

> *More scurrying around and then* GRAY *stops.*

GRAY (*offstage*). Sleep well?

ALICE (*offstage*). Yes thanks.

GRAY (*offstage*). Good.

ALICE (*offstage*). Why?

GRAY (*offstage*). You just seemed a bit . . . restless.

ALICE (*offstage*). You've got to go!

GRAY (*offstage*). Can I come back tonight, it'll be late?

ALICE (*offstage*). Call . . .

GRAY (*offstage*). . . . when I'm on my way, I know, I will.

> *He pauses.*

ALICE (*offstage*). What?

GRAY (*offstage*). Well?

ALICE (*offstage*). I'm not gonna say it just because you want me to.

GRAY (*offstage*). I know you do.

> *He rushes out in the dark.*

Love you . . .

ALICE (*offstage*). Yep.

> *Scene change:*

INT. SECURE UNIT – LATER

ANDREW *re-opens the screen. He fluffs up his pillow and sits neatly on the bed.*

ANDREW. I'm ready.

> HELEN *comes back in.*

HELEN. This is a lovely idea, Andrew.

ANDREW. Thank you, Helen. I can call you Helen?

HELEN. Of course.

ANDREW. I know you said you're not a therapist, but this is therapy, isn't it?

HELEN. If it's useful for you to frame it in that way, that's fine.

ANDREW. It's not useful.

HELEN. Are you suspicious of therapy?

ANDREW. It can fuck you up.

HELEN. As I said, I'm here to help you.

ANDREW. What did you mean by 'we have more in common than I think'?

HELEN *smiles that enigmatic smile again.*

You're doing that thing. Leaving a silence for me to fill. You know the police do that as well?

HELEN. It's only a technique.

ANDREW. One of many.

HELEN. Indeed. I actually prefer reciprocal disclosure.

ANDREW *is getting a bit frustrated.*

ANDREW. Sounds painful. What would you say we have in common?

He bangs his hands on the bed. HELEN *leans closer in.*

HELEN. You're quite forceful, aren't you?

ANDREW *goes quiet and introverted. He shuffles over to the other side of the bed. He grips his own wrist.*

I've noticed you do that too.

ANDREW. What?

HELEN. Hold yourself.

ANDREW. It's so I know I'm here. I want to stop now.

HELEN. That's understandable. But if you are able, try staying in that place of wanting to stop and listen to your feelings.

ANDREW *puts his hand to his ear.*

ANDREW. It really feels like I want to stop.

HELEN. Okay, when you were a child, what was the last thing you did before you went to bed?

ANDREW. You don't want to know.

17

HELEN. I do.

He looks genuinely troubled.

ANDREW. Alright! I went around my room putting everything in pairs.

HELEN. Good. What did you put in pairs, Andrew?

ANDREW. 'What did you put in pairs, Andrew?' Fucking hell, Helen.

HELEN. Yes?

ANDREW. You're pushing me.

He gets up and stands by the wall.

HELEN. I'll stop if you want.

He turns to her.

ANDREW. Toys, socks, pencils, you name it.

HELEN. That's it, good for you.

A beat.

Now, why in pairs?

ANDREW (*mumbling*). Before the lights went out, so nobody would have . . .

HELEN. I can't hear you.

ANDREW (*still mumbling*). So nobody would have to be on their own . . .

HELEN. I really can't hear you, Andrew.

ANDREW. . . . before he fucking came home from the pub.

HELEN. Your father.

ANDREW. Step.

HELEN. You're very brave.

ANDREW. I don't think so.

A beat.

I would lie there and suddenly see a sock on its own across the room and I would have to get back up and put it with another one.

HELEN. Why?

ANDREW. So it wouldn't be lonely on its own. Pathetic.

ANDREW looks in pain.

HELEN. No, it's very sweet.

ANDREW hones in on HELEN and sits close.

ANDREW. What do we have in common, Helen?

HELEN. I'm a recovering alcoholic too.

ANDREW. Ah, I get it, reciprocal disclosure. Brave of you. Thank you.

He rubs his head.

Can you see me again tomorrow, please?

HELEN. It's once a month.

ANDREW. Shame.

HELEN. How do you feel now?

ANDREW. Energetic.

HELEN. Good. And what have you learnt by living through your pain?

ANDREW *smiles.*

ANDREW. I'll get back to you on that one.

HELEN. Okay, I must go.

She moves to leave.

ANDREW. Helen, could you . . .

HELEN. What?

ANDREW. No. Stupid of me.

She's almost out of the door.

I would really like some music.

HELEN. Nice try, Andrew. You know the rules. If I could, I might, but I can't, so no.

ANDREW. I know, thanks anyway.

HELEN *leaves.* ANDREW *stands and looks at his wrist. He then holds it with his right hand before letting go. He repeats this several times like he's testing a scientific theory. He then closes the screen.*

Scene change:

INT. BEDROOM – NIGHT

With the screen still closed, a knock knocks.

GRAY (*offstage*). Alice.

ALICE (*offstage*). Er . . . err?

GRAY (*offstage*). Alice!

ALICE (*offstage*). Oh. Fucking hell.

GRAY (*offstage, shouting*). Alice!

ALICE (*offstage*). Gray! There's late and there's late. Fucking hell.

We hear her get up and then she angrily opens the curtain. GRAY *wobbles in.*

GRAY. Sorry, sorry. I know. I got held up.

ALICE. You got drunk.

GRAY. I might have had one.

She looks at him walking.

ALICE. So why are you slurring your legs? Did you call?

GRAY. Yes! It just rang.

ALICE. Just come to bed, please.

He starts to undress.

And you can leave your clothes on.

GRAY. Jesus, alright. I could have used my key.

ALICE. Please don't go on about that again.

He joins ALICE *in bed.*

GRAY. Me!

ALICE. Shush now. You stink.

He burps.

GRAY. Ah well. Night.

The lights fade.

And then fade back up to moonlight. ALICE, *oh so carefully, extricates herself from the bed. She then does something concealed with her hands and creeps off with almost comical stealth. As she approaches the back door, we can see a piece of string attached to her wrist and running back to the bed. She disappears around the corner.*

GRAY *stirs and instinctively, still mostly asleep, reaches out to* ALICE. *After a few pats, he wakes fully and sits up to see the negative echo of* ALICE's *vacated shape. He places his face on the sheet.*

Still warm.

He then spots the string and half-smiles.

What the fuck now?

Then he's up and with the string between his fingers, he traces his way through the back door. As he goes through the threshold, he almost bumps into HELEN *coming into the room. Neither acknowledge or, indeed, see each other.*

Scene change:

INT. SECURE UNIT, SESSION THREE – DAY

HELEN *enters the room. She looks at the empty bed. She then scans the rest of the room and checks her watch. She then moves to the bed and places her hand on* ANDREW*'s mattress and then quickly pulls it away like she's scolded herself.*

HELEN. Hot.

She then takes a CD out of her bag and furtively slips it under ANDREW*'s pillow. In doing so, she discovers a black-and-white photo. As she looks at it,* ANDREW *enters quietly behind her.*

ANDREW. Boo!

HELEN *jumps.*

Saw the picture then.

HELEN. Andrew.

They settle down on bed and chair.

How are you?

He looks troubled.

What's happened?

ANDREW. I'm worried.

She guiltily glances at the pillow.

HELEN. What about?

ANDREW. You writing to me, Helen.

She breathes out.

HELEN. Oh, I see. I thought it might be helpful.

ANDREW. Don't get me wrong, it was. Kind words, hopeful words.

He goes all teenage.

HELEN. What?

ANDREW. It felt . . . close.

HELEN. Okay . . .

ANDREW. Tender.

HELEN. Good.

ANDREW. Intimate though.

HELEN. That's me.

ANDREW. I just didn't know if it was allowed.

HELEN. It is, kind of.

ANDREW. I loved that exercise about peeling away a layer for each year of my life, until I arrived at childhood.

HELEN. Like the rings in a tree. Did you try it?

ANDREW. Yes. I followed a line as taut as a piano string back into my past.

HELEN. Do you know what a lovely way with words you have?

ANDREW. No.

HELEN. What did you find?

ANDREW. Something pure and small and . . . scared.

HELEN. Of?

ANDREW. Him.

HELEN. Was he violent?

ANDREW. Yes, he was.

HELEN. Towards you?

ANDREW. Emotionally, yes. Physically, no.

HELEN. He never touched you?

ANDREW. No. And that hurt more than his fists could ever have.

HELEN. That's an interesting interpretation.

ANDREW. Perverse, even. But he was clever in his cruelty. It was another way of leaving me out.

HELEN. Oh Andrew.

ANDREW. Let's not dwell. Now, when I did your exercise with the layers . . .

HELEN. Like a tree.

ANDREW. Yes, like a tree. Fucking hell, you lot love your trees, don't you? Anyway, I was surprised.

HELEN. You're amazing by the way. Surprised?

ANDREW is taken aback.

ANDREW. Thank you.

A beat.

Erm . . . by how easily I could discard all those intervening years, like I'd never lived them. It was me now and me then with just this thin, fifty-year-old piece of string in between.

HELEN. Wow.

ANDREW. Can we try something?

HELEN. I'm sure we can.

He guides her into position without touching her.

ANDREW. Can you stand there . . .

HELEN. Here?

ANDREW. Err . . . no . . .

HELEN. Here?

ANDREW. Not really. Sort of . . .

HELEN. Where, here?

ANDREW. Nearly.

They both chuckle at their mutual awkwardness.

HELEN. Here?

ANDREW. Almost . . .

HELEN. There?

ANDREW. There.

They are, by accident, now face to face and someone arriving in the room at that moment would almost certainly conclude they were about to kiss.

HELEN. You can touch me, you know.

HELEN *moves a little closer.*

ANDREW. No. I can't.

He skirts away and changes the subject.

After all was stripped away, all my middle life, I lay back on my bed.

He places his body against the wall.

And I looked up into the night sky. Then it happened.

HELEN. What did?

ANDREW. Shush. I could see myself as a child. And all that connected me now to me then was a blood-soaked umbilical.

HELEN. Are you there now?

ANDREW. Please. What I wanted to do was reel myself in. Pull down hand over hand. But I couldn't. It wouldn't work. I couldn't do it.

HELEN. Did you try?

He shoots her a look.

ANDREW. Of course I tried!

HELEN. Sorry.

ANDREW. The more I pulled down, the further I went up. Like a lost kite. You see, I thought I'd got somewhere, thought I had it, just for a second. But no, I realised. I'm not special, not a bit. Just one of the many, crying in the night.

He moves close to HELEN. *He looks utterly defeated.*

Enough to be going on with?

She attempts to put her hand on his shoulder but he jumps like a scolded dog. He moves back to the bed.

HELEN *feels, for the first time, a little out of her depth.*

HELEN. Did you have much physical contact as a child?

No response.

Erm . . . do you have brothers or sisters? No, I don't mean that.

A beat.

Did you feel rejected as a child?

ANDREW. These are not great questions, Helen, are they? This is not your best work.

HELEN. Did you feel responsible for what was going on around you?

ANDREW. I dunno.

HELEN. It's very common for a child to feel responsible when their world has no boundaries.

ANDREW. I'm gonna start calling you Trisha.

HELEN *attempts to get back on terms.*

HELEN. When I was a child, I did something terrible.

ANDREW *looks back to her.*

ANDREW. What, steal a brush from Woollies?

HELEN. Alright.

ANDREW. Sorry. Go on.

HELEN. When my little sister was born, I lost all the attention.

ANDREW. Big deal.

HELEN. SO . . . I tried to drown her.

ANDREW. Je-sus.

HELEN. I felt very bad about it for years.

ANDREW. I'm not fucking surprised.

HELEN. My sister's odd in the fact that she's never been able to ride a bike, she can't balance. And for years I thought it was all connected to those minutes she spent underwater.

ANDREW. Minutes!

HELEN gets out the big stuff.

HELEN. Who's in the picture, Andrew?

He looks hurt.

Who's in the picture, Andrew?

ANDREW. Can we leave that until next time? I don't feel very well.

HELEN. Sure?

ANDREW. I'm sure.

HELEN. Alright.

HELEN gets up to leave.

ANDREW. Thanks for . . . sharing with me, Helen. We have a connection now, don't we?

She smiles as she gets to the doorway.

HELEN. If you are a kite . . .

He claps his hands together.

ANDREW. Then you are my string!

HELEN. Yes.

ANDREW. Will you write?

HELEN. I will.

ANDREW sees her out like a born-again gentleman. He then returns to the bed and takes out his photo and the CD that HELEN secreted under his pillow. He weighs them in each hand. The CD appears to weigh more. He then pulls the screen across.

ANDREW. If I am a kite, then you are my string.

Scene change:

INT. FRONT OF SCREEN – NIGHT

Straightaway, ALICE appears around the front of the closed screen, with the piece of string still tied to her wrist. With her right arm pulled awkwardly back and facing out, she addresses the audience.

ALICE. Hello. Again. It's me, remember? Alice, or whatever the fuck you're called. I'll come clean. It's called . . .

She looks back.

Shuh! It's called parasomnia. It's a sleep disorder that interrupts or intrudes on my sleep. It's a derangement of arousal, partial arousal or what's called sleep-stage transition.

She pauses.

Sorry. Look, when you sleep, you dream. When I sleep, I dream. BUT. When you dream, you're paralysed. You don't know it but you are. This is important because it gives you the one, safe place to go insane. You don't act on it because you can't. When I dream, I skip the prostrate stage and jump in, feet first.

She looks closely at the audience.

I act out. I do dreams.

Another quick glance back. She gestures to the lead.

This is for sleepwalking. It can be dangerous. Especially if I go outside . . . and drive.

Another swift look behind her.

I better go.

She exits back around the closed curtain, leaving the string still trailing behind her.

From the opposite side, GRAY *enters, still pulling the string through his hands. As he gets centre stage, he gives the audience a withering look and shakes his head at his own actions.*

GRAY (*indignant*). What!?

He exits stage left behind the curtain. A brief pause follows before ALICE *once more totters around the front of the screen. As she makes her pass, she looks at the audience.*

ALICE. Sorry.

The moment she disappears, the screen starts to slide open from the other edge.

Scene change:

INT. SECURE UNIT, SESSION FOUR – EVENING

ANDREW *is opening the screen with a book in his hand. He sits and reads softly.*

ANDREW (*reading*). 'Many loves expire, some distressingly, some painfully and others bitterly. This does not mean that the overall effects were necessarily negative. Some ultimately failed affairs are enhancing while they last and the benefits to the lover may outlive the love itself. In love we reclaim parts of the self. But we buried them only because they had brought us so much pain.'

HELEN *enters.*

You're early. (*Reading.*) 'The energy set free when at last we feel loved, allows those long-buried parts of ourselves to flourish.'

ANDREW *looks up for the first time.*

By two weeks.

HELEN. Guess what?

ANDREW. What?

HELEN. I've managed to double our contact time.

ANDREW. Have you?

HELEN. Where would you like to begin, Andrew?

ANDREW. By thanking you.

They settle into their now familiar positions.

HELEN. For?

ANDREW. Not just another letter, but this book.

He holds it out to her like a bible.

HELEN. Have you found it useful?

ANDREW. Oh Helen, it's really good. I've read it twice. Some of it was like reading about myself. Me. Fuck. In a book, like my diary or something.

HELEN. Good. Now, shall we talk about the little girl in the picture?

ANDREW. You don't hang about, do you?

HELEN. Our time is precious, Andrew.

ANDREW. It is.

He gets off the bed and stands by the wall. A deep breath follows.

Okay. Nothing, no contact of any kind. Not even a note.

He turns to look right into HELEN'*s dark eyes. He strides towards her until all that separates them is a fluffed-up pillow.*

But. And this, sorry about my language, fucking kills me. She is the one entity I see last thing at night and whose lovely little lost face wakes me each morning.

HELEN *rides his emotional wave.*

HELEN. If you close your eyes and think of the one thing at the centre of all the things you want, what would that thing be?

He pulls the quilt up around him.

ANDREW. I would like to hold her.

HELEN. And if you think of the one pain, at the centre of all your pain, that is most painful?

ANDREW. I'm getting you now. Wow.

A beat.

It's the lack of any physical contact. To not be able to hold your child is a life lived like . . . like an obituary.

HELEN *is impressed.*

HELEN. Something's just crossed my mind.

ANDREW. Help me.

HELEN. Something that may seem . . .

ANDREW. I want to kiss her goodnight.

HELEN. I'll just say it. One of the techniques we could use is to create a safe environment in which to express your need for physical contact.

ANDREW. Uh?

HELEN. To create a pocket in which you can act out . . . with me, in a surrogate position.

ANDREW. I'm lost.

HELEN. Okay. I can passively play your daughter and you can act out your desire for physical contact with her.

ANDREW. Really?

HELEN. Yes.

ANDREW. Fucking hell. No.

ANDREW *moves well away.*

HELEN. I think you are kind and brave and a man with huge reserves of love.

ANDREW. Are you brave, Helen?

A beat.

Are you?

HELEN*'s turn to look confused.*

There's no way I can do this.

HELEN. When's her birthday?

ANDREW. Ouch!

HELEN. What?

ANDREW. 6th of June.

HELEN. A week's time.

ANDREW. I know.

HELEN. How many birthdays have you missed, Andrew?

He does a quick sum in his head.

ANDREW. Twenty-two.

HELEN. We can build up gently to this.

ANDREW. There's nothing gentle about this.

HELEN. What's her name?

ANDREW springs away.

ANDREW. Why?!

HELEN. Please sit down.

He slowly does.

Perhaps we could sing 'Happy Birthday' to her.

ANDREW looks angry.

ANDREW. Perhaps we could stop.

HELEN backs off.

HELEN. Alright.

He takes his time.

ANDREW. Luna. Her name's Luna. My lovely little Luna.

HELEN smiles.

When she was all tucked up, we had these two little things before sleep.

He stops.

HELEN. You're so close.

ANDREW. No, that is it. I can't do it.

HELEN stops.

HELEN. Listen to me, Andrew. You are so close but we will get nowhere if you persist in bailing out every fucking time something hurts!

ANDREW is genuinely shocked.

ANDREW. You're quite forceful, aren't you, Helen?

HELEN. Please.

ANDREW. What's this 'we will get nowhere'? I thought this was about me?

HELEN. A slip of the tongue.

ANDREW. Is this our first row?

HELEN. Choose your path, Andrew.

He summons up all his reserves of energy.

ANDREW. We had a rhyme and then a little ritual thing.

HELEN. Go on . . . I'm sorry.

ANDREW *folds over his thighs and closes his eyes.*

ANDREW.
One is for knowing love lifts you up the stair
Two is for padding softly into the night
Three is for stepping while brushing your hair
Four is for hugging and snuggling so tight

Five is for voices you know that care
Six is for teeth with a smile so bright
Seven is for waiting to hug your bear
Eight is for tomorrow, to fly your kite.

He unfolds himself and drops his head to one side.

You're crying.

HELEN. What was the other thing?

ANDREW. She would then kiss me four times here, here, then here and here.

HELEN. You can do that with me.

ANDREW. Why are you crying?

HELEN. You're crying.

ANDREW. Am I?

He wipes a tear away and looks at it on his fingertip, like it's not his.

Is that a tear?

HELEN. Do you want to kiss?

ANDREW. I want to kiss.

HELEN *stands and unconsciously turns her arms and exposes her wrists. She also closes her eyes.*

ANDREW *looks but then walks away.*

You swore, without hesitation, to tell me the truth.

HELEN *opens her eyes.*

HELEN. What? I will . . . I do.

ANDREW. Have a seat.

HELEN *ends up on the bed and* ANDREW *in the chair.*

Do you sing?

HELEN. What?

ANDREW. Do . . . you . . . sing?

HELEN. How did . . . why?

ANDREW. Do you always try and sing the harmonies?

HELEN. Uh?

ANDREW. Let me guess. Daddy left you . . . didn't he?

HELEN. Andrew.

ANDREW. He did, I know it. And then maybe . . . one Christmas in seven. Two birthdays in five?

HELEN. Where is this coming from?

ANDREW. I know what you did, Helen, we all would . . . tracked him down in your twenties. And with your heart in your mouth, you sat in that godforsaken KFC car park only to have it broken for a second time by his indifference?

She looks hurt.

HELEN. That's quite cruel.

ANDREW. I know, it's meant to be. How can I put this? Men are shit, Helen, hear me? The shittest. Lower than the low. They rarely have anything more to offer than their absence.

A beat.

They have departed hearts.

HELEN. People can change, look at you.

He holds her gaze.

ANDREW. And that is the biggest lie of all. If you place a thing at the centre of your life that lacks the power to nourish, you're fu . . .

HELEN. . . . fucked, I know. But look at you.

ANDREW. Good point.

ANDREW *goes for a little walk.* HELEN *takes a breather.*

So who have you replaced him with, Helen?

HELEN. Him?

ANDREW. Daddy.

HELEN. I'm not sure I understand the question.

ANDREW. Is there a man in your life?

HELEN. Oh Andrew. That's just not . . . anything.

ANDREW. I don't think that's very fair. I've opened up in the most painful way. You made me cry.

HELEN. That's the way it works. A clean slate . . .

ANDREW. . . . slate. I know. So what happened to reciprocal disclosure?

HELEN. There was a man but it didn't work out.

ANDREW. Go on.

HELEN goes into a completely black, staring-ahead, no-one-else-in-the-room world of her own.

HELEN (*flat*). Common-or-garden betrayal and deception. I was taken for a bit of a ride.

ANDREW. In what way?

HELEN (*flat*). Someone else had his baby.

ANDREW gasps.

ANDREW. Fuck! Everything's kids, isn't it. Kids, kids, kids.

HELEN (*flat*). It's alright. It was months ago.

ANDREW. So?

HELEN (*flat*). So . . . now my work is my focus.

ANDREW smiles.

ANDREW. There is a man in your life.

She slowly comes back to life.

HELEN. Who?

ANDREW. Me.

They both laugh.

HELEN. I suppose you're right. I should go. I'll see you next week.

ANDREW. Okay.

She takes a long time folding her chair up and then hovers in the doorway.

Bye then . . . what?

HELEN. See you then.

She turns away but still doesn't leave. Finally ANDREW jumps up.

ANDREW. Helen?

She answers a little too enthusiastically.

HELEN. Yes?

ANDREW. Can I give you this? It's Luna's details.

He holds out a piece of paper.

HELEN. For?

ANDREW. You could perhaps . . . no.

HELEN. No Andrew. I'm up to my neck in this, as it is. I can get you more music . . . more books, I'll write. But that's it.

ANDREW. Her phone number, that's all.

HELEN. No Andrew.

He thrusts the piece of paper in her hand anyway. She feels her fist close around it.

ANDREW. Can I have the theme tune from *Hill St. Blues* then.

HELEN *leaves.* ANDREW *is exhausted. He collapses onto the bed, causing it to complain. He picks up the book again, flicking through it manically. He settles on a page.*

(*Reading.*) 'Power and love would seem to be mutually exclusive. Even if someone of high prestige falls in love with someone lower, it is the very act of love that obliterates the power difference.'

ANDREW *gets up and absent-mindedly closes the screen, while continuing to read out loud.*

'Yet, despite this apparent disconnection between love and power, love is never completely free from the influence of power and many loves are corrupted by it.'

The closure is complete.

Scene change:

INT. BEDROOM – NIGHT

ALICE *opens the curtain almost straightaway with the string going from her wrist all the way back into the doorway. It suddenly tightens, pulling her arm slowly back.*

GRAY *enters, holding the other end and for a moment they stand, silently linked by the thin line.*

ALICE *then jumps out of her skin.*

ALICE. Fuuuccckkkk! No, no.

She tears the string off.

Get out of there. Don't go in there. The door. The light's on down there. Turn it off.

GRAY *just stares.*

No! It's getting brighter. Turn it off, turn it off.

GRAY. What can I do?

She pushes him violently forward.

ALICE. Get down there and close the door.

GRAY. Where?

ALICE. Can you not see?! THERE!

GRAY is overwhelmed.

GRAY. I don't see.

ALICE. It doesn't have a lock . . . it's swinging open . . . please, oh no! Close the door before it's all out. PLEASE . . . THERE!

GRAY. Here?

ALICE. There.

He walks across the room.

There.

GRAY. Okay, look . . . I get it.

He mimes it for her.

It's closed. All done.

ALICE *seems satisfied and gets into bed.* GRAY *follows. The lights fade.*

The distant, amplified sound of a phone being dialled and then ringing comes from offstage. HELEN *speaks from off, while* ALICE *talks while apparently still asleep.* GRAY *is dead to the world.*

ALICE. Gray . . . I was aslee . . .

A beat.

Who's that?

HELEN (*offstage*). Erm, sorry . . .

ALICE. For what . . . ?

HELEN (*offstage*). . . . for calling you so late. This is going to sound a bit odd. A bit of a shock perhaps.

ALICE. Is it? What is?

HELEN (*offstage*). All of it.

ALICE. Listen, I don't know who you are, so go away.

HELEN (*offstage*). Wait . . . wait! No, hold on, I understand. But just hear me out.

ALICE. Leave me alone.

HELEN (*offstage*). Is Luna there?

ALICE *takes a while to answer.*

ALICE. Who?

HELEN (*offstage*). Luna . . .

ALICE (*monotone*). You have the wrong number you have the wrong number.

HELEN (*offstage*). Are you sure?

ALICE (*monotone*). You have the wrong number you have the wrong number.

HELEN (*offstage*). Are you Luna?

ALICE. You have the wrong fucking number.

HELEN (*offstage*). Okay, I'm sorry. Can I leave you my number anyway?

ALICE. For what?

HELEN (*offstage*). 07740 954 695, that's 07740 954 695. I'm really sorry to have disturbed you.

ALICE. Leave me alone.

She's then up and away to the door, appearing to look for answers and anchors and things to cling to like she fears levitation. She's drawn, gaunt and not quite present and becoming increasingly preoccupied with the mimetic action of trying to unlock imaginary, locked doors. GRAY *sits up.*

GRAY. Alice! It's five o'clock in the fucking morning.

ALICE. It's a door.

GRAY. There's a surprise.

ALICE. It has yellow glass in it.

GRAY *reluctantly climbs out of bed and shadows her.*

GRAY. Is it locked?

ALICE. Of course it's locked, my fault. I can go here, but not here. Just there but I can't turn down there.

GRAY. Why not?

ALICE. Cause that's locked. Yale, they're all Yale. I'll try here.

She moves some more and then turns on GRAY.

What are you doing?

GRAY. What?

ALICE. That's a wall, you can't walk through a wall. Stay behind me.

Off she goes again.

GRAY. Where are you now?

ALICE. The top of the stairs.

GRAY points to the real open door.

GRAY. There.

ALICE. Yes!

GRAY starts whispering.

GRAY. Can you go down?

ALICE. I don't know!

GRAY. Shall I go first?

ALICE. You go first.

He moves further.

GRAY. Here?

ALICE. Why are you whispering?

He catches himself.

GRAY. I've no idea. Shall I go down?

ALICE. Yes! I'll wait at the top.

GRAY steps very slowly.

GRAY. Is this right?

ALICE. Be careful, please be careful.

GRAY. Am I alright here?

ALICE. Oh God . . . a little bit more. The bottom, to the left, there. The door with the light under it. There . . .

GRAY. Here?

ALICE. THERE!

GRAY. Further?

ALICE looks terrified.

ALICE. Oh . . . oh. Oh God . . . please.

GRAY. What? What!

She completely loses it.

ALICE (*screaming*). Oh my. NOOOOOOOOOOOOOOOOO! NOOOOOOOOOOO!

GRAY flies back to her.

GRAY. It's alright. Look, I'm coming back up, all the way up.

ALICE lurches towards him.

ALICE. Fucking hell. Fucking fuck. You do the practice. You do the practice. You do the rehearse!

GRAY. I don't . . .

ALICE. The plan, the plot, the steps, the set-up. Stupid.

GRAY is clueless. He holds his hands up in frustration.

GRAY. I don't know what you mean, Alice.

ALICE. The draft, the design, the diagram. The fucking map you misfit. (*Screaming.*) Do I really have to spell it out for you?

She shoves him away and then launches herself, back to the wall.

Super trouper.

GRAY. Eh?

ALICE. Shut up!

She takes one, deliberate step towards the bed.

Beams are gonna blind me. (*Another step.*) But I won't feel blue. (*Another.*) Like I always do. (*Another.*) For somewhere in the crowd, (*Another.*) there's you.

She arrives at the bedside and goes torpid.

Suddenly I feel alright. And it's going to be so different, when I'm on the stage tonight.

She then throws herself onto the bed, screaming.

FUCKFUCKFUCK. Leave her alone. What have you done?!

GRAY rushes over. She pushes through him to get back into the other side of the bed.

GRAY. Leave who alone? Alice!

ALICE. I'm sleeping now. I'm asleep and I'm not listening to you. I need to sleep and you are stopping me, so shut up and let me sleep!

GRAY. Alice!

ALICE. Not listening.

GRAY. Tell me who is hurt.

She grabs hold of his head. With each line, she jags his head back.

ALICE.
One is for sudden, sharp sit up and listen
Two is for tippy-toe down the stair
Three is for handprints of colour that will glisten
Four is for dirty hands tattooed in hair

Five is for fear of opening the door
Six is for breathless, standing stony still
Seven's for voices screaming to the core
Eight is for knowing the weight of a will

37

Nine is for knowing we can't take no more
Ten is for knowing love waits beyond the door.

She manhandles him out of the door.

Shut up and go away. Leave me alone, get out!

She then wraps herself in the quilt. She sits shaking for some time before a quiet whisper appears to calm her.

Nine is for knowing we can't take no more
Ten is for knowing no love waits beyond that door.

She runs out, almost knocking ANDREW *over, coming the other way through the doorway. A letter that was in his hand goes up in the air.*

Scene change:

INT. SECURE UNIT, SESSION FIVE – NIGHT

ANDREW *slumps down on the cold floor with the letter in his hand. He reads out loud.*

ANDREW (*reading*). 'Dear Andrew, I hope this letter finds you in good spirits and that your quest for a happier life is moving in your chosen direction. However, it is with a heavy heart that I bring you difficult news. After a great deal of soul-searching and much painful discussion with my team leader, I have taken the agonising decision to . . .

ANDREW *audibly gasps and visibly stiffens. He drops the letter and grips his triceps. Only after a near panic attack has been avoided, does he pick up and read on.*

. . . taken the agonising decision to . . .

A beat.

Terminate my visits. I realise I have crossed a line and broken a bond for myself, my organisation and most critically, for you. I have allowed my personal feelings to cloud my professional judgement and this is unacceptable. I wish you well on your brave journey and have nothing but admiration for your courage. Yours, Helen.'

He pulls out the photo and then folds it into the letter before dropping them to the floor. He then curls up in a ball and covers himself in the quilt.

From within the cocoon of the quilt, ANDREW *can hear muffled heels approaching.*

That really better not be you.

In she comes.

HELEN. I'm so sorry. This must be confusing for you.

ANDREW. This is confusing, Helen.

He throws off the bedding and looks her up and down. She looks like she always does but something's not quite right. Nothing he can put his finger on but something has changed.

I'm hurting, Helen, can you not see that? And I'm the last person in the world who needs any more messing around with.

He stands.

Why? Why do this to me?

She's mute.

Hey? You know I have issues, great fat fissures and fractures.

He offers her the insides of his forearms.

Arterial wounds that will not stop pumping. I am unbelievably fragile, Helen. And then you do this?

She holds up her forefinger and thumb.

HELEN (*imploring*). I made a little, tiny, minuscule error of judgement. One.

ANDREW. And . . . ?

HELEN. Another . . .

ANDREW *shapes like he's describing the big fish that got away. He tries to support her through this difficult time.*

ANDREW. Then a bigger one . . .

HELEN. Yes! And another. Then it . . . it just snowballed. All I'm trying to do now, is to make it better.

ANDREW. You can't backtrack, Helen, none of us can. Infidelity is an action in gear, not a neutral thought.

HELEN. I don't . . .

ANDREW *pounces on the paper on the floor. He holds the photo under her nose.*

ANDREW. See this? This. See her? A young woman now, forbidden from knowing her own dad with a mother who disinvented him for the sake of her own slim life.

He drops to the floor.

Frozen, in a suspension of memory, Super Eight and Polaroid.

He points both index fingers at her.

You are just like the rest of them. Like her and her and her and like them all.

HELEN. I got you *Hill St. Blues.*

He jumps up laughing hysterically.

ANDREW. What! Brilliant. Thank you from the bottom of my broken heart.

He strides away, putting the maximum distance between him and HELEN.

HELEN. I called Luna.

ANDREW *stops like he's walked into an iceberg. Life freezes but then thaws.*

ANDREW. How do you know it's her.

HELEN. It's her.

ANDREW. So you have her number?

HELEN. Yes.

ANDREW*'s mood vaults polarity in an instant. He's suddenly bouncy and jubilant.*

ANDREW. Can you come back tomorrow?

HELEN. No.

He raises an eyebrow.

Yes.

ANDREW. Yes. Tomorrow. Your phone, her number . . .

They're nose to nose.

And a drink . . .

HELEN *pulls away.*

. . . to celebrate.

HELEN *protests as* ANDREW, *still with no physical contact, shepherds her out the door.*

It's alright, don't worry about things you can't control. We all fuck up from time to time.

He walks back in.

It's how you deal with it.

He bounces back in and dances and skips around every square foot of his room.

One is for knowing love lifts you up the stair
Two is for padding up into the night
Three is for stepping while brushing your hair
Four is for hugging and snuggling so tight

He throws his bedding and mattress across the floor, kicking it up into the air in a blur of delight and anticipation.

Five is for voices you know that care
Six is for teeth with a smile so bright
Seven is for waiting to hug your bear
Eight is for tomorrow . . .

ANDREW *hurls a pillow case high into the audience.*

. . . to fly your kite.

He then joyously draws the screen closed.

Scene change:

INT. BEDROOM – NEXT DAY

The curtain opens by itself. ALICE's bedroom looks like a burglary victim. Mattress off, the bed frame like a broken tooth and bedclothes cast asunder.

In the far corner the quilt stirs, as ALICE slowly crawls out from under it. She gets to her feet like a newborn giraffe – all weak legs and wet neck. She takes a moment to survey the scene, before thudding back down in the middle.

GRAY *reveals himself from behind the bunched curtain.*

GRAY. Well, fuck me, morning Alice.

She says nothing and keeps her back to him.

Sleep well? I didn't . . . in the bath.

ALICE. Sorry.

GRAY. I think you've got some explaining to do.

ALICE. What did you see?

GRAY. You're telling me you don't know?

ALICE. I was asleep, Gray.

GRAY. Asleep?

ALICE. It's all part of it.

GRAY. All of what?

ALICE. It's called parasomnia.

GRAY. Good name, abnormal sleep. That doesn't quite do it justice.

ALICE. It's a disorder that intrudes on my sleep. A derangement of arousal, partial arousal or what's called sleep-stage transition.

GRAY. Thank you, doctor.

ALICE. I act out. I do dreams.

GRAY rubs his head.

GRAY. I know. I came back from the loo to find you in a garden.

ALICE. Really?

GRAY. SodaStream? Heather Trim? A swing near a window? Lupins!

ALICE. Really?

GRAY. Oh, and the tent peg/Tampax axis.

ALICE. Oh . . . yes.

GRAY moves around to her.

GRAY. Why didn't you tell me? All that stupid rehearsing. All that 'You will call?'

ALICE. Alright.

GRAY. It's no good hiding.

ALICE. I tried to protect you.

GRAY. I'm a big boy, Alice. I can take it.

He sits down beside her.

ALICE. Didn't work out that way with the others.

GRAY reacts indignantly.

GRAY. Do I look like the others?

She looks at him for the first time.

ALICE. You do, actually.

GRAY tries to laugh.

GRAY. Are you serious?

ALICE. Was it the same?

GRAY. Same what?

ALICE. Was I a child again?

GRAY. Yeah, I think you were.

ALICE. Was it really bad?

GRAY gets up and almost involuntarily starts to act it out again.

GRAY. Top of . . .

ALICE. Stairs?

GRAY. Yeah.

ALICE. Fuck.

GRAY. We, well . . . I went down. I tried to help and then I . . .

ALICE jumps up.

ALICE. Hold on, stop. You went down?

GRAY. Yes.

ALICE. You tried to help? Me?

GRAY. Yes!

ALICE. Why?

He thumps the wall.

GRAY. Give me fucking strength, Alice! BECAUSE . . . I . . . LOVE YOU.

ALICE. That's your problem. What did I do?

GRAY. Okay. Super. Trouper.

ALICE. Shit.

GRAY. How long has this been happening?

ALICE. What else was there?

GRAY. Do you think you should, I don't know, get some therapy or something?

ALICE. Ha.

GRAY. Well?

ALICE. Gray, stop a moment. Was it?

GRAY. You need help, Alice.

ALICE. Gray?

GRAY. I'm not set up for this.

ALICE. Gray!

GRAY. What!

ALICE. Was it . . . ?

He just looks.

The . . .

His eyebrows say 'come on . . . '

. . . the . . .

GRAY. Say it.

ALICE (*excruciatingly embarrassed*). One is for tippy-toe down the stair.

GRAY. Oh yes.

43

ALICE folds up.

Hurt who, Alice?

ALICE. I don't know what you mean.

GRAY. Okay, what about the house?

ALICE. Which house?

GRAY. It was so specific.

ALICE. I really don't want to talk about it.

GRAY. Was that your house?

ALICE. That's the house.

GRAY. Where you grew up?

ALICE. Yes!

GRAY. Alice, hurt who?

ALICE. Will you fucking leave it?

GRAY. Hurt who, Alice?

ALICE. I don't know!

He moves to the bed.

GRAY. You should have warned me.

ALICE. What did you expect, Gray? Oh hello, I'm an amazing sack artist but sorry, you'll get no sleep because I'm as mad as an Alpine postman.

A beat.

Well?

GRAY goes for a little walk.

GRAY. It's worse than having a fucking baby.

ALICE. Like you'd know.

GRAY looks validated and hurt all in the same expression. ALICE's face drops even further.

No?

GRAY. You should ask ME about ME sometime.

ALICE. Are you telling me you have a child?

GRAY. Tell me about your dad, Alice.

ALICE freezes.

ALICE. Where the fuck did that come from?

GRAY. I'm just asking the question.

ALICE. You're just asking WHAT question?

GRAY. You tell me.

ALICE. Fuck off.

GRAY. We've got to this point SO many fucking times. And then you just clam up. If we have a future, you have to let me in!

ALICE. Please stop.

GRAY. What is it with your fucking childhood that makes you so special, anyway?

ALICE. Gray! Enough . . . enough!

GRAY. You're not the only one with a back story.

ALICE. Stop it!

GRAY. Daddy not love you? Join the queue.

ALICE. Please.

GRAY. Mummy too busy? Throw a stick an you'll hit six.

ALICE. Stop.

GRAY. And lovers like a string of fake pearls.

ALICE. Bastard.

GRAY. One of the many.

ALICE. Shut up!

GRAY. And why won't you ever tell me that you love me?

ALICE studies him and takes her time. The air sucks out of the room.

ALICE. Because I don't.

Much to his surprise, GRAY finds the wall sliding up his back until he feels the floor rising to meet his bony arse.

GRAY. Good point.

ALICE. Can you go now, please?

GRAY. I don't want to.

ALICE. Can you go now, please?

GRAY. Alice.

ALICE. Can you go now, please?

GRAY. I'm not someone who backtracks.

ALICE. Can you fucking go now!

GRAY. Why?

ALICE. I have someone to see.

GRAY. That's that then.

He walks away.

ALICE begins to re-assemble her room. She awkwardly drags the mattress back onto the frame. It screeches a high-pitched protest as she drags it back into place. The linen and quilt are last. She sits on one side.

Then ANDREW enters and takes his place on the other side of the bed, delineating two separate worlds on a lethal trajectory. After much deliberation, ALICE exits, leaving ANDREW on his own.

Scene change:

INT. SECURE UNIT – SESSION SIX

HELEN enters, a bit unsteady on her pins. Her appearance has deteriorated some more. She has a 'Bargain Booze' carrier bag which she dumps in the centre of the bed. She then sits on the front edge.

HELEN. It's done.

ANDREW. Good.

ANDREW dives into the bag and takes out a three quarters' full bottle of vodka.

Very good.

Next the phone.

HELEN. Fully charged.

ANDREW. The number?

HELEN. It's in there, under . . .

ANDREW. L.

ANDREW laughs. He then moves around to sit next to HELEN.

HELEN. It's done.

ANDREW. It's done.

HELEN. I suppose I should fuck off now.

HELEN really laughs. ANDREW sees her laugh and raises her. It goes back and forth, with the stakes increasing expeditiously. He mirrors the action from their earlier meeting.

Seriously though, what now?

ANDREW continues to laugh.

I could fit another session in next week?

He smiles.

Or I could just hang around for a bit now?

ANDREW. Can we try something?

HELEN. Yes please.

ANDREW. Stand there a second.

HELEN. What here?

HELEN starts to giggle.

ANDREW. No, here.

HELEN. You sure you don't mean here?

ANDREW. No, here.

HELEN. Sure you don't mean . . .

ANDREW. There.

HELEN. There . . . where? Here?

ANDREW. There.

They are face to face once more. They both laugh again. Surely it's time for their long-awaited kiss.

HELEN. You can touch me, you know.

ANDREW. Helen . . . I . . .

HELEN. And I love you too.

But no. ANDREW *delivers an utterly sickening, fat-fisted punch to her stomach. She hinges at the waist like a broken door, gasping for breath like the back has been knocked out of her. He then throws her hard at the wall.*

ANDREW. FUCK OFF!

ANDREW *stands over her.*

Listen, love, it's over, all done. You've been helpful, if a little . . . childlike in your enthusiasm. But I've done with you now. So fuck off.

He stalks away and sits with his back to her on the bed. Then like a deer disturbed in the woods, he tenses, stands and looks back to HELEN, *who is still fighting for breath and is now close to vomiting her womb.*

(*Completely calm.*) Did I not just tell you to fuck off?

He flies back at her.

I get it. Something's just . . . crossed your mind. What's real? What's true? Common-or-garden betrayal and deception. Surely I haven't been taken for a ride . . .

He grabs her neck.

AGAIN!

He gets face to face with her and flips like a coin, appearing to calm completely.

(*Tender.*) Ask me about my childhood?

HELEN *is too fucked to breathe, let alone speak.*

Go on, I'm in a hurry . . . you know, call to make?

He smiles.

Argh! You're doing that silence thing. Please, quickly, come on.

She forces it out.

HELEN (*monotone*). Tell me about your childhood.

He goes from nought to nuts in less than a second.

ANDREW. NO! You tell me! YOU TELL ME!!!

She tries.

HELEN. You put things in pairs . . .

ANDREW *backs off and stalks around.*

ANDREW. I was quite proud of that one. So they wouldn't be alone, like me. Oh yes, very good. What else?

HELEN. I don't know.

ANDREW *hits a new high of aggression.*

ANDREW. YOU DO!

She tries to swallow herself.

HELEN. Layers . . . peeling away . . . the layers.

He really laughs.

ANDREW. Yes, you tree-hugging fucking state. What was it? Blood-soaked umbilical. Yeah, I liked that.

He slaps her around the head.

So did you! 'Do you know what a lovely way you have with words, Andrew?' That was a good one.

He gets closer again. More pathetic, female impersonation.

'What can you see, Andrew, what can you see? Like a tree, Andrew, like a tree. I'll be your string, you be my kite. You are the wind beneath my wings.'

He stalks away, exploding verbally.

Do your fucking research, Helen. Your book, you soppy cunt. Page 28, chapter 15.

He heads back to the bed.

See what you've done to me? Fucking hell! Driven me back to the drink.

He holds up the bottle to her.

Not the only one by the look of it. I'll tell you what. It's a good job I'm not angry.

He cracks open the vodka and takes a big swig. HELEN is pathetically sliding along the wall, trying to get out of there. ANDREW jumps up and cuts her off, then slams her back to the floor. He then sits beside her.

Sorry. Really. Fuck. Lost it there for a minute, didn't I?

He holds her head close to his in all seriousness.

Do you think it's passed on, Helen?

HELEN *forces her eyes open.*

HELEN. What?

ANDREW. What? Fuck me, come on!

HELEN. There's evidence for both.

ANDREW. Get off the fence.

HELEN. Yes . . . I do . . . don't know . . . maybe.

He kisses her on the head.

ANDREW. And what have you learnt by living through your pain?

HELEN *spits on the floor.*

HELEN. I. Don't. Know. It's too much for me.

ANDREW. That's good, Helen. Knowing your limits. Knowledge is like an expanding balloon; the more you know, the greater the surface area of what you don't know. As I'm sure you now know.

ANDREW *relaxes his grip and* HELEN *starts to slug towards the door again.* ANDREW *pulls her back by her hair.*

Come here. You're shaking. Let's share. You need a drink.

He flips again.

Have a drink! Have a drink, Helen. HAVE A FUCKING DRINK!

He swigs a mouthful and then snogs her hard on the lips. Vodka gushes all over her face and down her neck.

There you go.

Another mouthful which he spits in her face. She chokes and spits and curls up. It's truly awful. He stands and grabs her hair and drags her to the door.

Just like the rest of them. All done now, path chosen, goodbye. I need to make a call.

He drags her outside.

Scene change:

INT. SECURE UNIT – CONTINUOUS

ANDREW *then thunders back in and collapses on the bed, trying to regulate his breathing.*

ANDREW. Every fucking woman in my life . . .

He then sits up with a start and looks at the audience.

Oh, hello. Did you see that . . . all of it?

A beat.

What?!

He gets up and stands very close to them.

My mum saw his medical records by mistake. It said he was a paranoid alcoholic with schizophrenic tendencies resulting in disruptive episodes. Disruptive episodes? God bless the fucking medical profession. The question I'm asking is, is there anything I could have done to avoid the trajectory and crude weight of my own sick lineage? Is there anything I could have done to . . .

Over his shoulder, footsteps and then a shadow extends into the room. ANDREW *stiffens. He doesn't look around.*

(*To the audience.*) Ohhh no! Tell me she's not back for more. (*To the figure behind him.*) That . . . really better not be you.

The figure stops in the doorway.

Did I not just tell you to fuck off!

ALICE *reveals herself.*

ALICE. Not me you didn't.

ANDREW *spins around and then simply cannot believe his eyes. He finally blurts.*

ANDREW. Alice? Happy birthday?

ALICE. Are you kidding? The 6th of October, October! It's fucking June.

ANDREW. You sure?

ALICE. Of course I'm fucking sure, it's my birthday.

ANDREW. So, how's tricks?

ANDREW takes a step towards her.

ALICE. Stay right where you are.

He does. She sniffs the air.

Have you been drinking?

ANDREW (*rushing*). If I close my eyes and think of the one pain, at the centre of all my pain, that is most painful, I think of you.

She just looks at him.

(*Rushing.*) If I close my eyes and think of the one thing at the centre of all the things I want, I want you. To not be able to hold you is a life lived like an obituary.

No response.

I'm doing all I can to help myself get well . . . and I'm allowing others to help me in that goal.

ALICE. Will you shut the fuck up! Why didn't you stop me?

ANDREW. Stop you what?

She stamps her foot.

ALICE. You know precisely what I mean.

ANDREW. That.

ALICE. Yes, that.

ANDREW. I did my best, all I could. I carried you. I took you away, out of harm's way. You chose to come back.

ALICE. I chose, did I? I was six years old. I was a child.

ANDREW takes another step and holds his arms out.

ANDREW. Yes, my child.

ALICE. Oh, fuck this.

She turns her back on him.

ANDREW. Why come then?

No reply.

Do you need help?

No reply.

Are you in trouble?

Still no reply.

Have you got boyfriend trouble, Luna?

ALICE. Don't call me that.

ANDREW. That's it, isn't it? How sweet, you've come for advice.

ANDREW *is on a roll.*

Let me guess. It's all going great. You're getting closer and he's telling you how much he loves you and every day is a new bunch of lilies and every night is the 5th of fucking November.

A beat.

And all he needs are those three little words. And then?

A beat.

You can't say it. And why?

ALICE *moves to him and for the first time realises why.*

ALICE. Because I still love you.

ANDREW *beams.*

ANDREW. Because you still love me.

For the first time in twenty-nine years, a dad brushes a strand of hair off his daughter's face.

Every night I've tried to picture you, what you must look like.

He pulls her close.

ALICE. Stop.

ANDREW. A anagram of Daddy and Mummy. My nose. Her eyes. My heart.

ALICE. Please stop.

His eyes scan ALICE's *wrist and then follow a thin, purple highway to the inside of her elbow. He holds her close.* ALICE *is falling into* LUNA.

ANDREW. Like a vein, I run through you.

Fully under the spell, LUNA *drifts and then falls into her past.*

ALICE. Quickly now! Through the door. I have the key. Over here . . . listen.

ANDREW *looks embarrassed and stays close to the wall.*

ANDREW (*reluctantly*). What?

ALICE. Shush!

ANDREW. What, Alice?

She looks slowly around at him.

LUNA. Who? Who is this Alice? I am Luna. You call me Luna. Ask me where I am.

ANDREW. Where are you, Luna?

LUNA. I'm in my bedroom sitting upon my new continental quilt, can't you see? Ask me how old?

ANDREW. How old?

LUNA. I am in my bedroom and I am six.

ANDREW. And?

LUNA. Be quiet. There, put your ear down. Listen . . . something's happening. You've started. One is for . . .

ANDREW. One is for knowing love lifts you up the stair . . .

LUNA. No, that's wrong.

ANDREW. We did it together.

LUNA. No. All on my own.

She looks back down to the bare floor and then jumps back a pace.

And one is for sudden, sharp sit up and listen. Oh no.

ANDREW (*impatient*). What?

LUNA. I hear it starting. It must be eight . . . there, oh please no. The music's starting. From the music centre.

It is. A subterranean version of Elvis's 'Spanish Eyes' creeps up through the boards.

Will it be tonight? Will it happen again, tonight?

She takes a tentative step.

I have to go down now . . . oh . . . please no. Have to go down there now . . .

She moves silently to the right, with ANDREW *reluctantly in tow.*

Okay, okay. Right, ready. Two is for tippy-toe down the stair. Little steps, little silent pads . . . down we go down we go. The stairs, the carpet is not to the edges and has little hard bars across it. We have to stay in the middle, the soft part with our socks.

They both walk along a preordained path and move three steps across. LUNA *suddenly sits down hard, holding her head in her hands.*

Oh, please don't, please, she sees it, she sees it. I can see it! Three is for handprints of blood that will glisten.

She lurches forward and then jumps at the wall, scraping the palm of her hand along it.

Oh, it's coming alright. We must go through the door without delay. To see it all with eye's witness.

She turns back and grips ANDREW's *hand and after jumping the final, imaginary three steps, dives into what was the front room. They both bundle in and then* LUNA *freezes, utterly still and staring.*

ANDREW. No! I will not do this.

LUNA *turns very slowly to face him.*

LUNA. You did it you do it you do it you did it.

ANDREW *holds his head.*

ANDREW. Fucking hell.

LUNA. Do it do it do it.

ANDREW. What then?

She begins to shake.

LUNA (*disembodied*). There is a sideboard with one door open. There are shiny bottles inside of it with Advocaat in letters on it. There is a music centre on top of the sideboard. You built it yourself with unclean hands out of wood. 'Kentucky Rain' is a song and the wallpaper is, you said, flock. Everything smells of plastic apples. Four is for . . .

ANDREW. Four is for hugging and snuggling so tight.

LUNA. No, no. Four is for dirty hands pulling at hair.

She rushes back out of the room in her head and stands facing front.

The door is all broken bits yellow glass. I am too young to understand but I am very good.

She pushes through the door and into the cold and dark garden. She then drops to her knees, looking at her hands.

There are pieces of hair in my hands because I am on your back and you are on top of her, pulling her hair as I am pulling yours.

ANDREW *looks shocked.*

ANDREW. I'm sorry.

LUNA. You are so gentle to me. I am up and away but I am too young to understand but am very good. I am being carried through the broken glass like a special doll.

She sits down on the floor at the feet of the audience.

Never would hurt me, I am his special Luna, his lovely Luna. His little angel Luna. I am his special Luna.

She hears him approaching.

And you put me on the kerb so gentle and then watch you walk away and you are so sweet and kind and big and brave and next door are trying to hold me back. They are number forty-seven who have a party phone line with us, seven four three double six. And the door is closed now and the sounds have started again and it's soft and hard and wet all in a one'er and they are all looking at me like I can do anything to stop and a new word I am taught which is big letters and three bits and spells do-mes-tic and they walk away and don't not even a coat in the rain with my knickers.

ANDREW *attempts to hold her.*

ANDREW. Luna, honey . . .

She thrashes out at him, then runs back to the bed.

LUNA. No. No honeys! No the honeys. No the loves. I am going back in now to the door with the sign on it.

She traces a well-rehearsed route with ANDREW *just a step behind her.*

I have one way to walk in the house from my room to the kitchen with the new tumble dryer and the extension with my handprint in the wet cement, waiting you said, to go off. One way to walk because all the other doors are locked with Yale because I lied and said it was not me when I boiled the kettle dry on the new Formica work-top. And that time when I lost Mummy's money in the Co-Op field and you said, 'Luna, you are nothing but a fucking liar,' and I am, through and through, a fibber and I did shame. And I did and I did and I found your magazines in the wardrobe and I deserve it and I am so sorry for it all. Five is for fear of opening the door with another word that is not big but means big which is private and the noise still happens and then it stops and I am opening the door.

She then looks back to ANDREW.

And why would she let it happen? Why didn't she stop it? Why? She has it too. We all have the blame and shame. Can you tell me why? She can't – with the red stuff all dripping and you without clothes with that thing hanging between your legs and feet red and splashes on the big mirror and our settee with thick drips like stalactites.

A beat.

And her . . .

She sinks to her knees.

And her . . .

No stopping the tears now.

Her, mine. Oh my. My mummy. Broken in the head with a white pillow case with pink jelly and snot bits and lots more red.

A beat.

An I look up an you look down. An I look up an you look down.

ANDREW *is standing over her in that exact position.*

An you look sad so sad with eyes like my favourite dobber. (*Blinking.*) And I want to kiss you and say how very sorry I am and I will never ever do it again, again. Ever, ever.

ANDREW *cannot watch.* LUNA *runs back around the bed.*

But I can't because the men with voices coming out of their chests have come and they put us all in separate rooms and from then on I am not allowed to touch you or her or even see and say a word like sorry or even goodbye.

She drops to her knees.

Because . . . they say you've done murder on my mummy.

ANDREW *is crushed.*

ANDREW. I don't know what to say, Luna.

ALICE *is very matter of fact.*

ALICE. Who is this Luna? I'm Alice.

ANDREW *starts to fade away.*

Little girls will always, always love their daddy. It's the size, the scale. Their strength. But I am a woman and you are a fuck head . . .

As ANDREW exits, ALICE continues to speak, but to herself as she climbs into bed.

. . . and the years of copying the negative space you left me with are over. No more surrogates. No longer the look-a-likes. An end to heat without warmth.

Scene change:

INT. BEDROOM – MANY MORNINGS AFTER

ALICE *is alone and asleep. A single shaft of clear winter light weds beam to blind to bed.*

GRAY *enters holding two cups of tea and a tea-cake with a candle in it. He watches ALICE sleeping, before moving to her.*

GRAY. Honey . . . honey?

She stirs a little.

Happy birthday to you,
Happy birthday to you,
Happy birthday, dear Alice,
Happy birthday to you.

You want some tea, sweetheart?

She wakes properly and looks at him for a long time.

ALICE. Yeah, I love you.

GRAY *almost drops the tea.*

GRAY. What?

ALICE. I said I'd love some.

They share the edges of a smile as GRAY joins her on the bed. They then fold into each other and under the quilt.

Suddenly ALICE and GRAY fly back up and out of the quilt with a huge, bloodcurdling scream.

Aaarrrgghhh!

GRAY (*simultaneously*). Aaarrrgghhh!

She looks at him, he at her.

ALICE. You are . . .

GRAY. Joking?

ALICE. Yeah.

GRAY. Yeah.

ALICE. You too?

GRAY. Yeah, sorry.

ALICE. Good one.

They both lie back down.

GRAY. Good one.

ALICE. Gray?

GRAY. Yeah?

ALICE. Thanks . . .

GRAY. For?

She beams and lets the moment hang.

ALICE. The tea.

Fade to black.

The End.

A Nick Hern Book

The Night Shift first published in Great Britain as a paperback original in 2005 by Nick Hern Books Limited, 14 Larden Road, London W3 7ST in association with Fuel

The Night Shift copyright © 2005 Mark Murphy

Mark Murphy has asserted his right to be identified as the author of this work

Typeset by Country Setting, Kingsdown, Kent, CT14 8ES
Printed and bound in Great Britain by Bookmarque, Croydon, Surrey

A CIP catalogue record for this book is available from the British Library

ISBN-13   978 1 85459 893 6
ISBN-10   1 85459 893 7

CAUTION   All rights whatsoever in this play are strictly reserved. Requests to reproduce the text in whole or in part should be addressed to the publisher.

Amateur Performing Rights   Applications for performance, including readings and excerpts, by amateurs in English (and stock companies in the USA and Canada) should be addressed to the Performing Rights Manager, Nick Hern Books, 14 Larden Road, London W3 7ST, *fax* +44 (0)20 8735 0250, *e-mail* info@nickhernbooks.demon.co.uk, except as follows:

Australia: Dominie Drama, 8 Cross Street, Brookvale 2100, *fax* (2) 9905 5209, *e-mail* dominie@dominie.com.au

New Zealand: Play Bureau, PO Box 420, New Plymouth, *fax* (6) 753 2150, *e-mail* play.bureau.nz@xtra.co.nz

Professional Performing Rights   Applications for performance by professionals (except stock companies in the USA and Canada: see above) in any medium and in any language throughout the world should be addressed to Kate McGrath, Fuel, BAC, Lavender Hill, London SW11 5TN, *fax* +44 (0)20 7228 6688, *e-mail* info@fueltheatre.com

No performance of any kind may be given unless a licence has been obtained. Applications should be made before rehearsals begin. Publication of this play does not necessarily indicate its availability for performance.